Good Manners in Relationships

Good Manners with Your Friends

by Rebecca Felix
illustrated by Gary LaCoste

Magic Wagon

visit us at www.abdopublishing.com

Published by Magic Wagon, a division of the ABDO Group, PO Box 398166, Minneapolis, MN, 55439. Copyright © 2014 by Abdo Consulting Group, Inc. International copyrights reserved in all countries. All rights reserved. No part of this book may be reproduced in any form without written permission from the publisher.

Looking Glass Library™ is a trademark and logo of Magic Wagon.

Printed in the United States of America, North Mankato, Minnesota.
102013
012014
The book contains at least 10% recycled materials.

Text by Rebecca Felix
Illustrations by Gary LaCoste
Edited by Stephanie Hedlund and Rochelle Baltzer
Interior layout and design by Renée LaViolette
Cover design by Renée LaViolette

Library of Congress Cataloging-in-Publication Data

Felix, Rebecca, 1984-
  Good manners with your friends / by Rebecca Felix ; illustrated by Gary LaCoste.
      pages cm. -- (Good manners in relationships)
  Includes index.
  Audience: Age 3-10.
  ISBN 978-1-62402-025-4
  1. Etiquette for children and teenagers--Juvenile literature. 2. Friendship--Juvenile literature. I. LaCoste, Gary, illustrator. II. Title.
  BJ1857.C5F37 2014
  395.1'22--dc23
                                                    2013028880

Contents

Why Do Good Manners Matter with Friends? 4

Show Good Manners with Friends! 10

Manners in Motion 24

Amazing Facts about Manners with Friends 30

Top Five Tips for Good Manners with Friends 31

Glossary 31

Web Sites 32

Index 32

Why Do Good Manners Matter with Friends?

Hazel invited her friends Tyler and Jen over. They planned to watch a movie. Then they would play board games. Jen arrived first. She and Hazel began talking about the fun day ahead. Then Tyler arrived. Should Hazel keep talking with Jen? Or should she go greet Tyler?

KNOCK KNOCK

Hazel should excuse herself from Jen. She should say hello to Tyler. Greeting friends makes them feel important and liked. It also makes them feel welcome. Greeting friends is one way to show good manners. Good manners are important in friendships.

When you visit a friend's home, it is polite to also greet their parents.

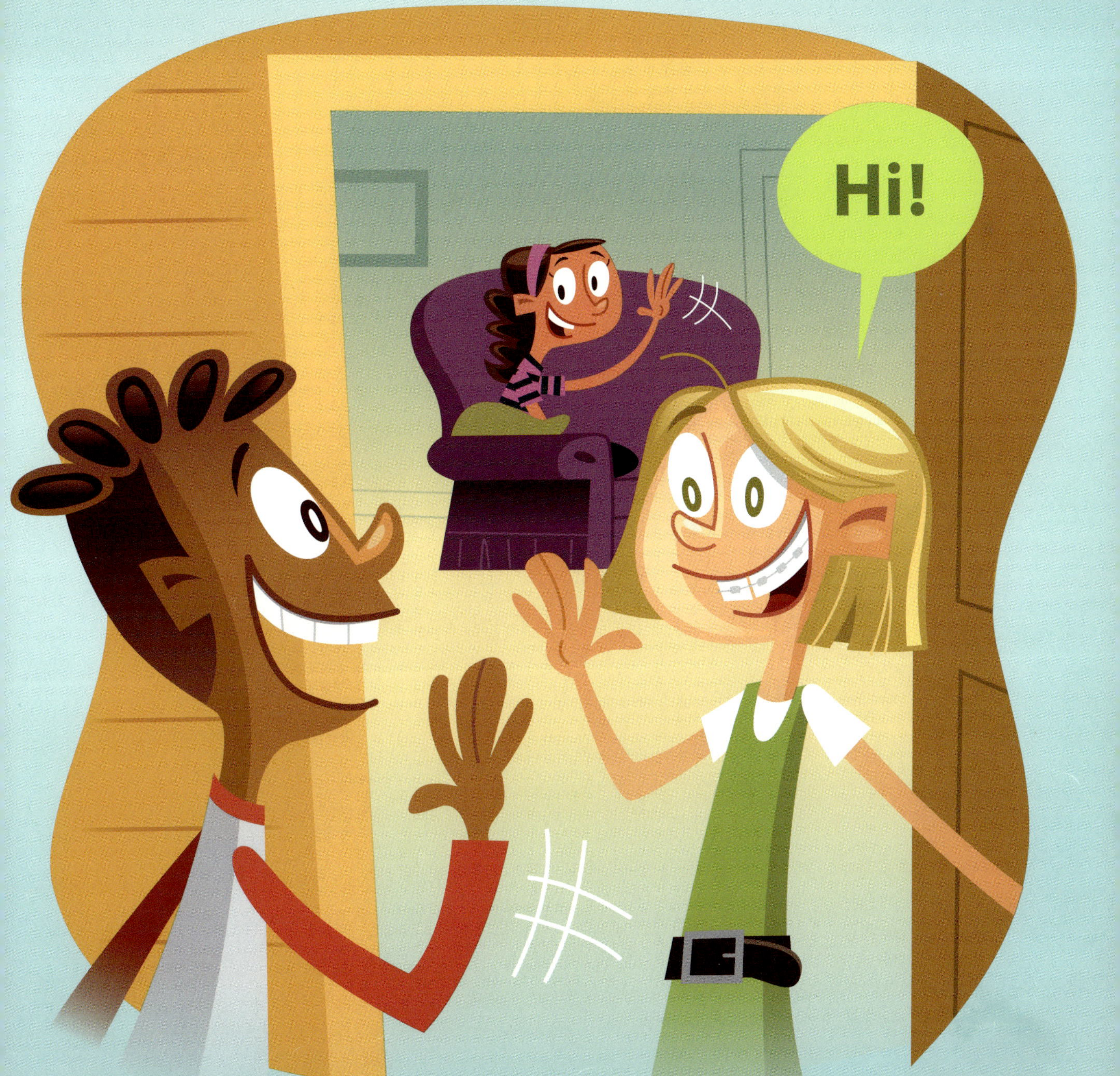
Hi!

What would friendships be like without good manners? Hazel might ignore Tyler, making him sad. Then she might laugh at Tyler for feeling sad. Jen might talk over Hazel. All three friends would probably get upset. Friendships might even be ruined.

9

Show Good Manners with Friends!

Using good manners helps friends enjoy spending time together. The base of good manners is respect. Respect means treating someone how you would like to be treated. It means listening and being polite. Treating friends with respect shows you care about them. What other manners are important in friendships?

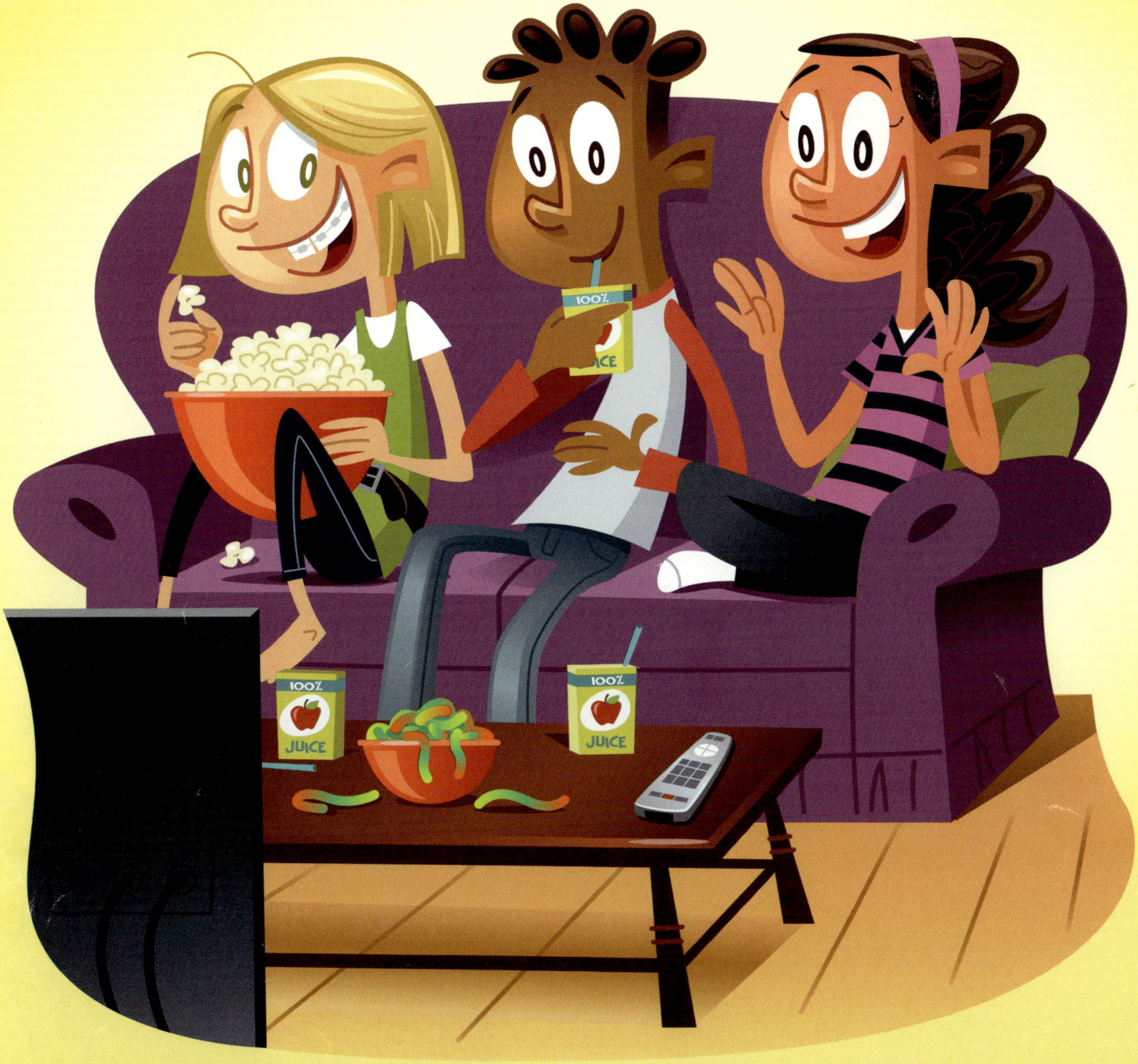
100%
JUICE
100%
JUICE
100%
JUICE

It is good manners to talk politely to friends. Use the word "please" when asking a friend to do something. While watching the movie, Jen can ask Hazel to please pass the popcorn. "Please" is a "magic word." It makes friends more likely to help you, and to feel happy doing so.

Magic words are small, easy words to add to conversation. But the positive difference they make is huge!

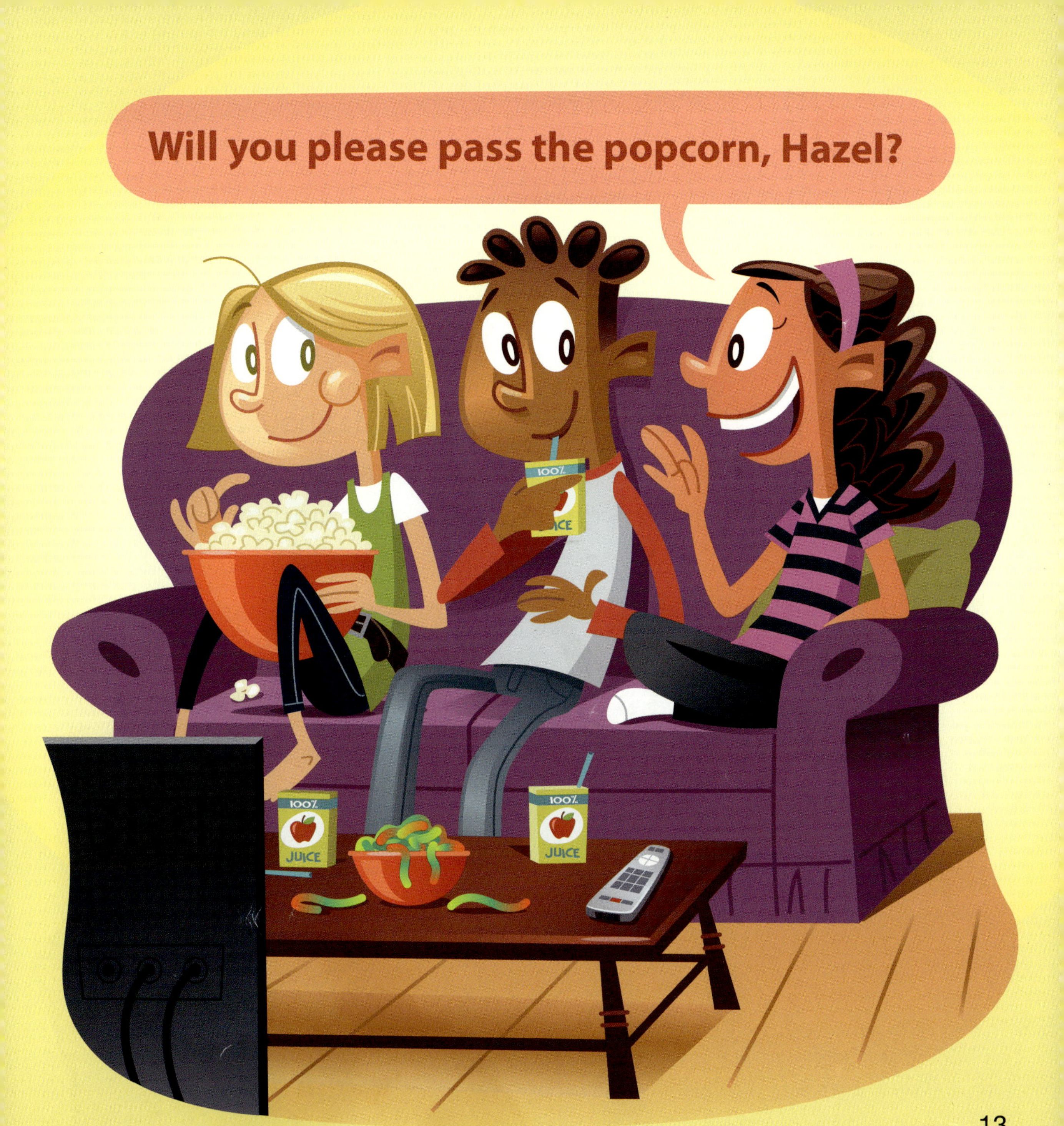
Will you please pass the popcorn, Hazel?
100%
JUICE
100%
JUICE

"Thank you" is a set of magic words. It should be used when a friend helps out. It should also be used when a friend gives a gift or says something nice.

Saying "thank you" shows you appreciate a friend's actions or words. Jen should thank Hazel for passing the popcorn. When Tyler tells Hazel she chose a great movie, Hazel should say "thank you!"

The polite response when someone tells you "thank you" is to say "you're welcome."

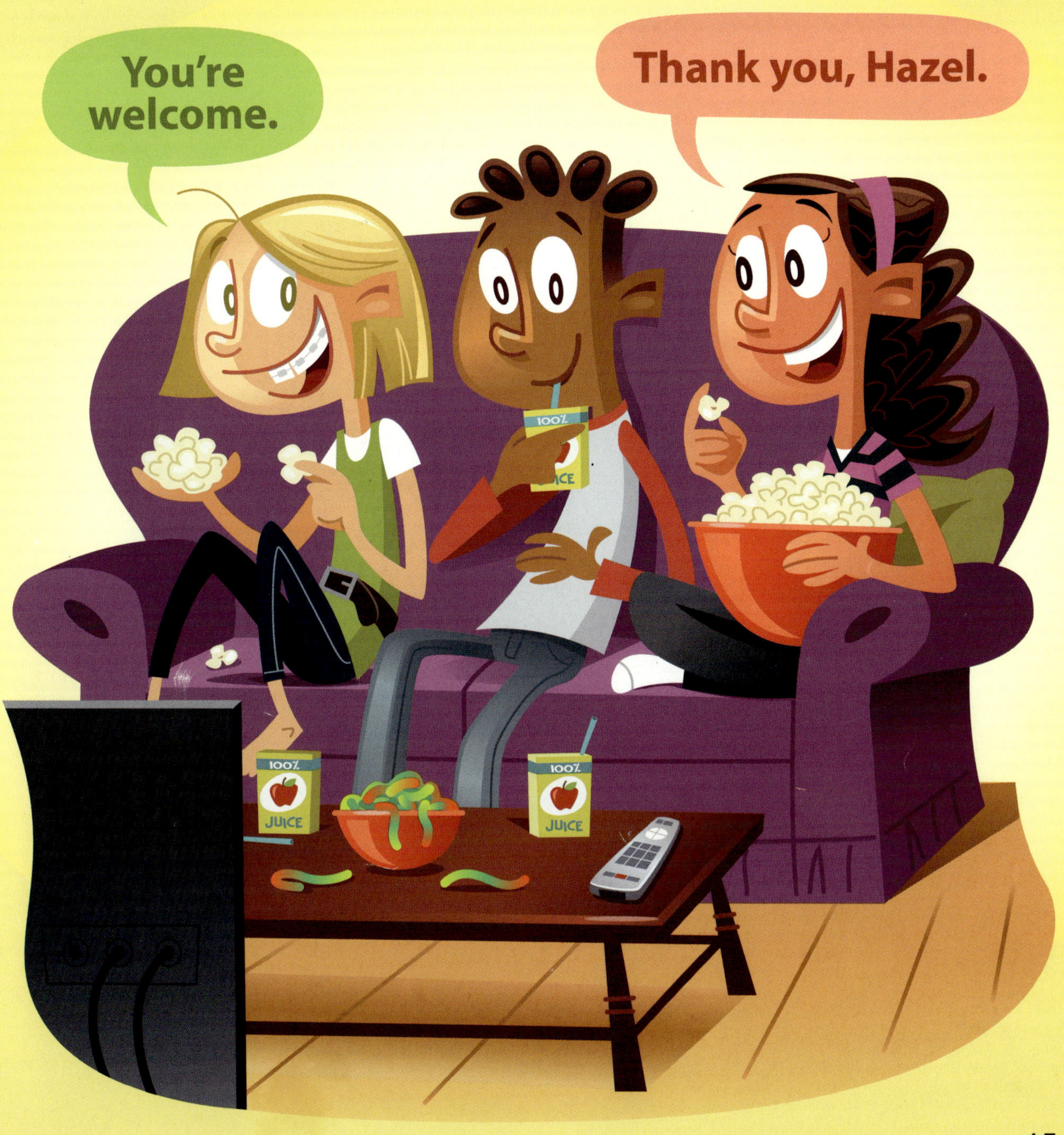
You're welcome.
Thank you, Hazel.
100%
JUICE
100%
JUICE
100%
JUICE

Hazel set out gummy worms to eat during the movie. They are her favorite treat! But it would be rude to eat them all herself. She should share with Jen and Tyler. This will show that Hazel wants them to enjoy the treat, too. Not sharing is greedy. It can make friends upset. It may even cause a friendship to end!

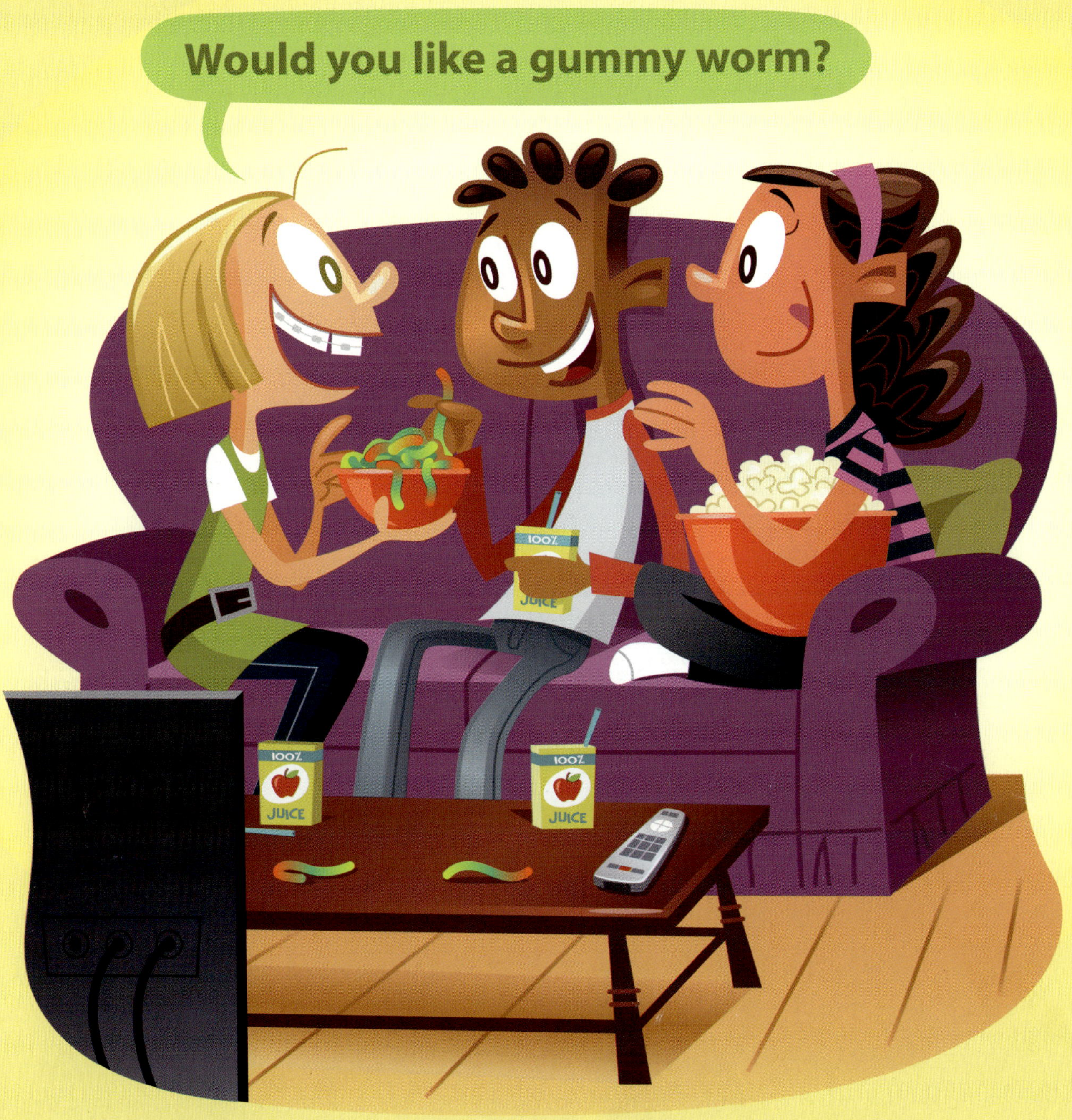
Would you like a gummy worm?
100%
JUICE
100%
JUICE
100%
JUICE

After the movie, Jen, Tyler, and Hazel all want to play a different board game. What game should they play? They should take turns playing each game. Taking turns shows friends what they want to do matters. It is also good manners to take turns being first.

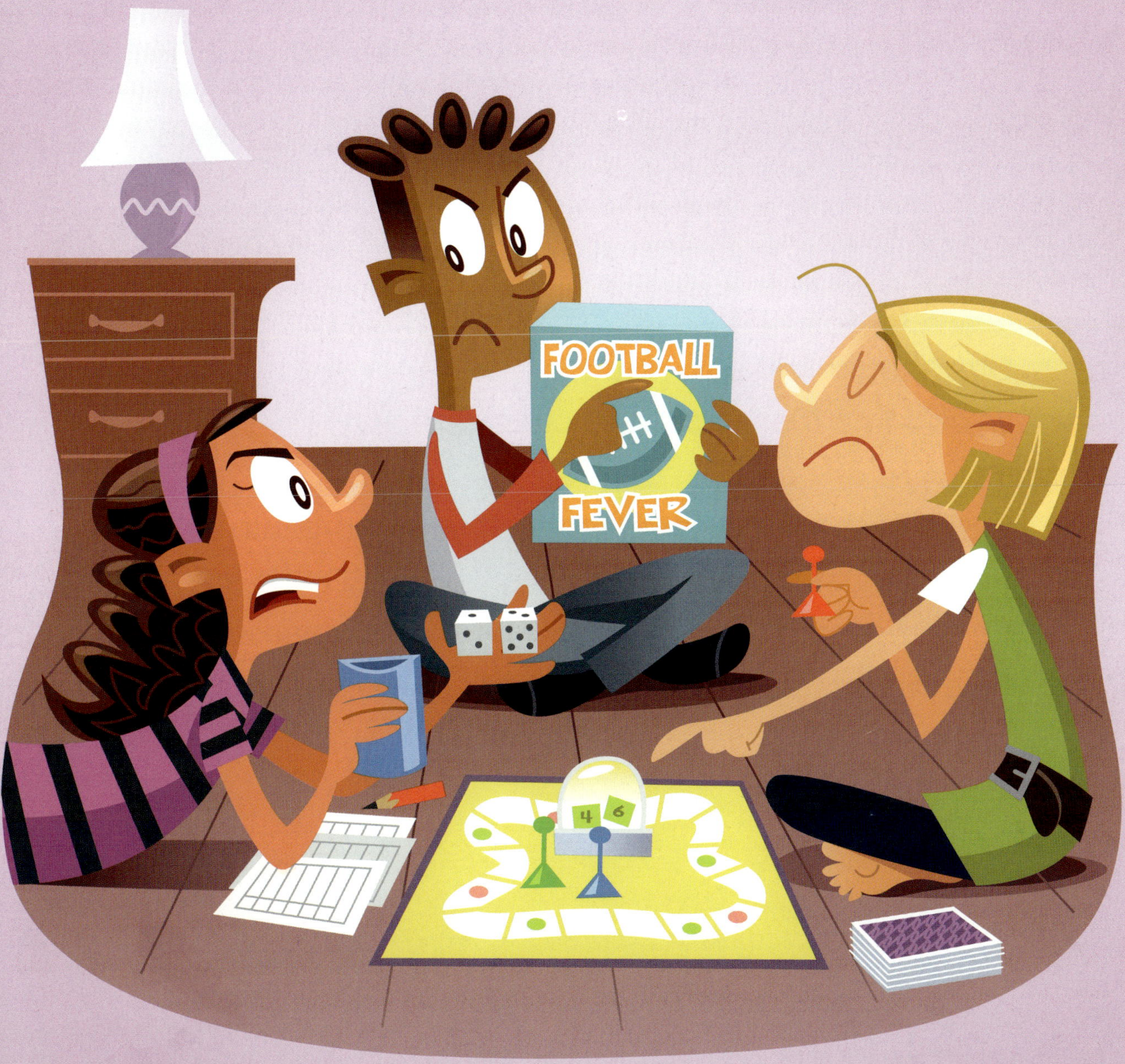
FOOTBALL
FEVER

Hazel reaches past Tyler to move her game piece. She should first say "excuse me!" This is a nice way of asking a friend to move out of the way.

It is also the polite thing to say if you bump into a friend. Tyler moves out of Hazel's way. Doing so, he bumps into Jen. Tyler should say "excuse me." This will let Jen know that bumping into her was an accident.

"Excuse me" should also be said after a burp. This tells people the burp was an accident.

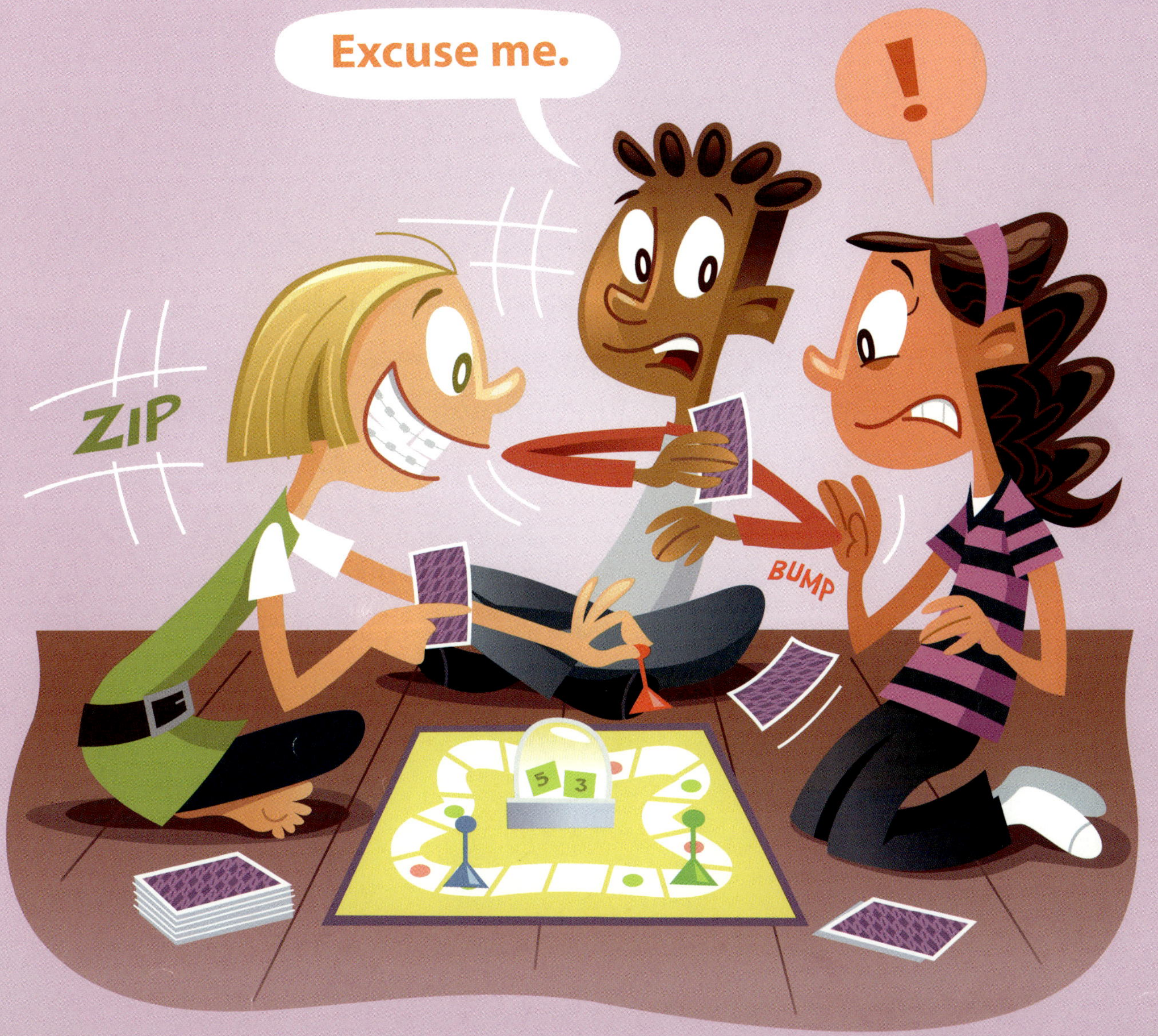
Excuse me.
!
ZIP
BUMP

Everyone has accidents and makes mistakes. Friends might say something silly or wrong. Friends like different things. It is good manners to be kind in these situations. Being kind shows friends that their feelings matter.

What if Hazel teased Tyler about the game he liked? Or if Jen laughed at Hazel when she spilled soda? This behavior would be mean. It would not show good manners. Now get ready to see some good manners in motion!

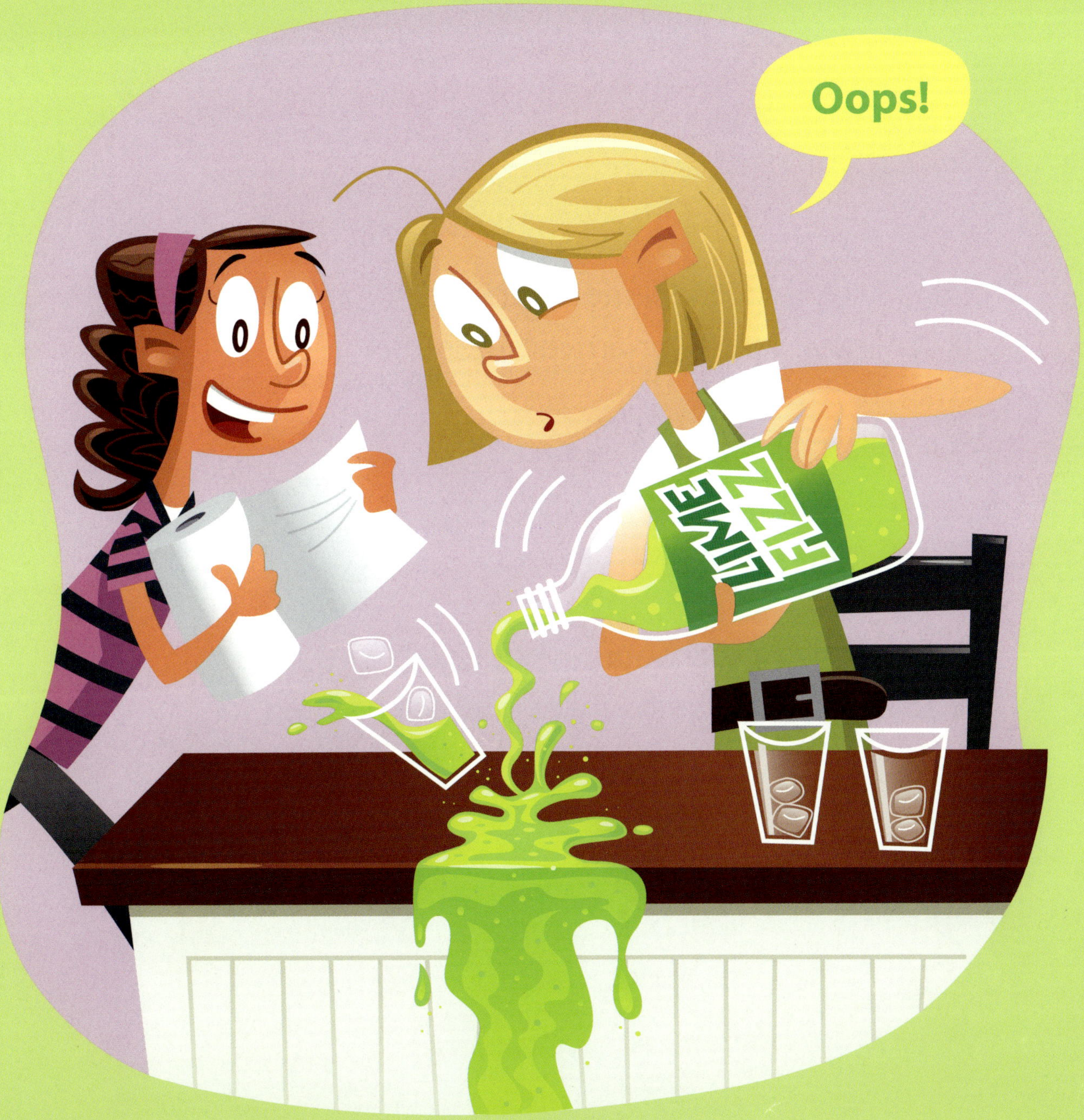
Oops!
LIME FIZZ

Manners in Motion

Jen, Tyler, and Hazel met at the park. Jen arrived first. Hazel and Tyler arrived together.

"Hi, Tyler! Hi, Hazel!" Jen said.

"Hey, Jen!" they said.

The friends talked about what to do first. Hazel wanted to play catch. Tyler and Jen wanted to swing.

"Let's take turns doing each!" Hazel said. Everyone agreed.

25

The friends played catch first. Then Hazel pulled a bag of gummy worms from her pocket. Her friends had liked them during the movie. So, she brought them as a gift.

"Thank you!" said Jen and Tyler.

"You're welcome," said Hazel.

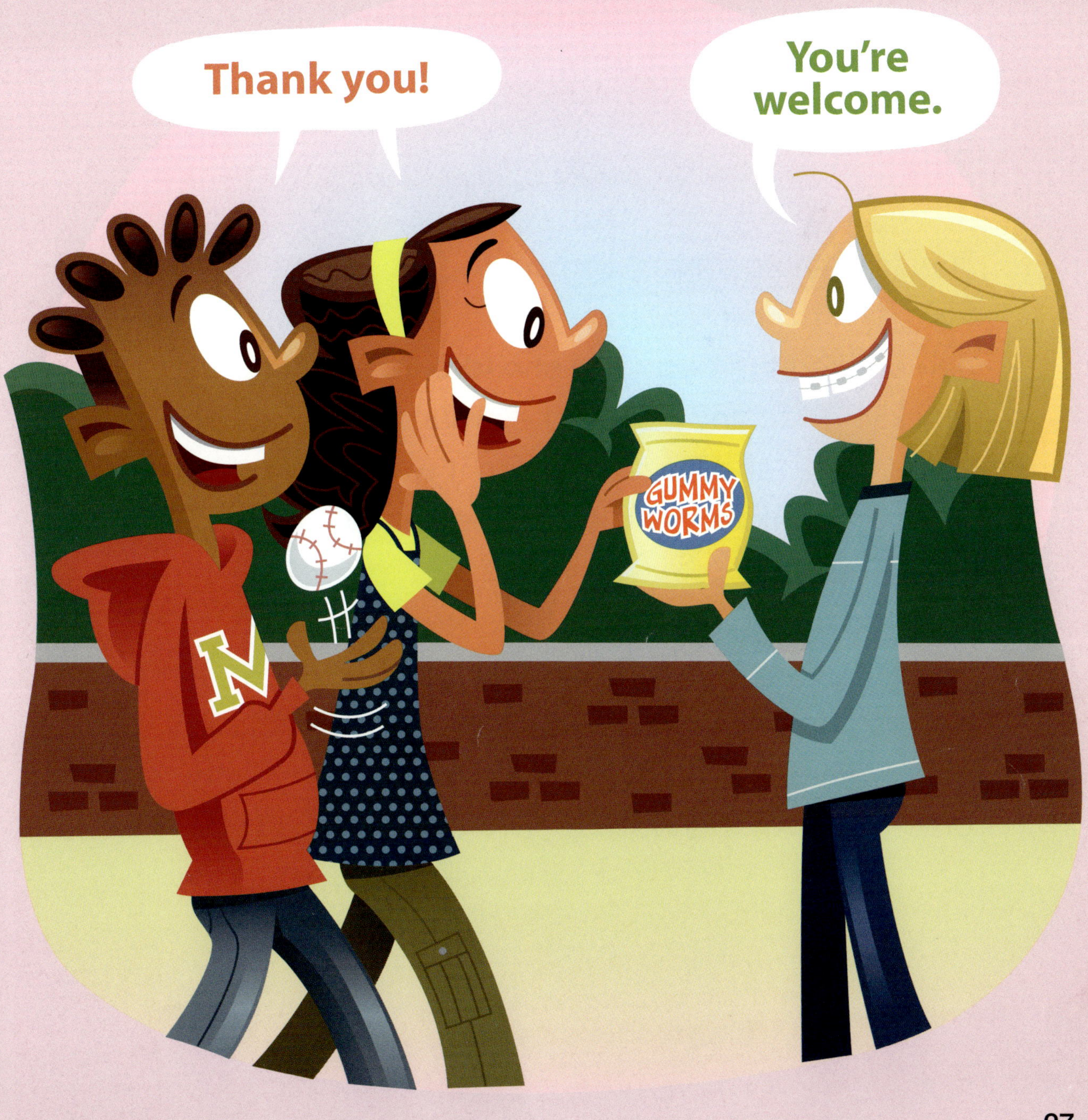
Thank you!
You're welcome.
GUMMY WORMS

"Let's all share them," Jen said.

Jen opened the bag. But she tore the package too quickly. The candy fell to the ground. Jen looked upset. Tyler and Hazel told Jen it was no big deal. Then they helped her pick up the candy.

How did Hazel, Tyler, and Jen show each other good manners? They were polite and kind. Treating friends this way is easy! Just remember to show friends respect. What good manners have you practiced with friends lately?

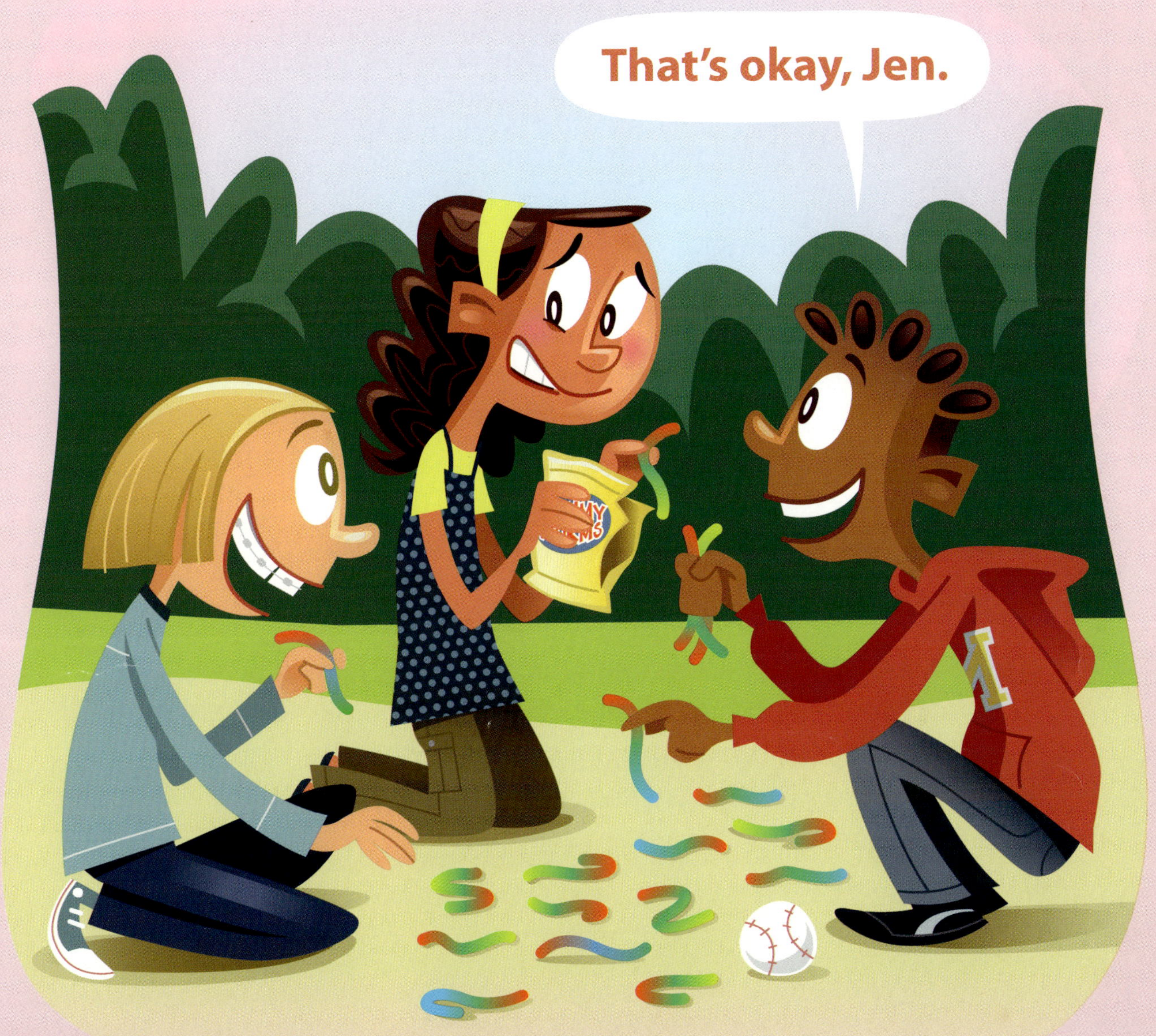
That’s okay, Jen.

Amazing Facts about Manners with Friends

A World of Greetings!
Saying hello is a polite greeting in the United States. So is hugging or shaking hands. Cultures around the world use different greetings. Certain tribes in New Zealand rub noses. Some East African tribes pretend to spit at a friend's feet as a greeting! Other cultures bow. Some kiss a friend's cheeks to say hello. Good manners are important in all cultures. Using cultural greetings shows respect.

Show Friends Good Manners Online!
Good manners should be used with friends online. Be sure to greet friends and say good-bye. Write politely. It is also polite to use your real name online. Always show friends respect online. Do this by keeping whatever they share with you to yourself.

Top Five Tips for Good Manners with Friends

1. Be kind.
2. Treat friends with respect.
3. Share.
4. Take turns.
5. Don't forget to say "please," "thank you," and "excuse me!"

Glossary

appreciate — to recognize and be thankful for something.
greet — to make eye contact and say hello.
polite — showing good manners by the way you act or speak.
rude — showing bad manners by the way you act or speak.
situation — the event of a certain moment.

Web Sites

To learn more about manners, visit ABDO Group online at **www.abdopublishing.com**. Web sites about manners are featured on our Book Links page. These links are routinely monitored and updated to provide the most current information available.

Index

accidents 20, 22
being kind 22, 28
being polite 10, 12, 20, 28
excuse me 20
greeting friends 4, 6, 24
ignoring friends 4, 8
laughing at friends 8
listening 10
mistakes 22
please 12

respect 10, 28
rude 16
sharing 16, 26, 28
taking turns 18, 24
talking over friends 8
teasing friends 22
thank you 14, 26
you're welcome 26